3 LEV

OF

FEMININTY™

with 9 Therapeutic based Art

Activities to Assist your

Ascension

By

Olive Swan

CONTENTS

PREFACE

Normally, a book like this would be written in this fashion:

Chapter 1 Girly

Chapter 2 Sensual

Chapter 3 Spiritual

But not this book, it's not that I had to be different, but it happens to be different. The book just formed this way, as it was being birthed from my spirit. It is written by topic instead and all the levels are discussed within each topic.

I did not research, copy, imitate, google, nor repeat this information from any person, entity, or physical source; this came directly from revelation from the Holy Spirit, and time spend with Him, along with study of the female nature, and observation of women over time. This is new and fresh, at the very least to me and I hope to you to, since I have not heard anyone share or speak about this subject in this manner, anywhere else. This is one of the manifold beautiful things about the

Lord; if you are faithful, He will show you 'new' things that no one knows yet. This is also scriptural. (See passages here: Deuteronomy 29:29, Jeremiah 33:3, Daniel 2:22, Amos 3:7, I Corinthians 2:9-10).

Please interpret this information not as a debasement, but as a radar and an assessment of truth. We all must experience childhood then adolescence, and next adulthood. We all have different periods of growth and development. Our transitions are all not alike nor do they come at the same stage and the same way of experience as others. Accept your journey and always aim for higher, better, and finer ways of living life. Timing of progress, shifts, and transformation is individualistic; it is based on, but not exclusive to, God's Appointed Times and You: Your Energy, Your Environment, Your Desire, Your Drive, Your knowledge, Your Decisions, and Your Actions.

Examine this: Have you ever bought anything that says 100% of the contents inside? Did you know if you put a little bit of something else with it, it's no longer 100%? Even if you put a tiny bit of something, like .0005%, it's still not purely 100%. Appropriately, that's the same with femininity. There's femininity and then there's diluted versions of femininity.

Think of the well-known chemical formula of H_2O, which represents Water. If you change the compound to HO_2, you get Hydroperoxyl instead. If you switch around the same components, you get very different results. Changing the elements of femininity evolves into an anomaly, a deviation, a mutation and it's not pure femininity.

Each level of femininity has its own ingredients. The purest and highest form of femininity is unmixed, unpolluted, and unchanged from its original form. It can be smelled, tasted, felt, heard, and seen. Masculine men can sense immediately and subconsciously, if a woman has feminine attributes or not, as well as which level of femininity she is in, even though he is not feminine. A truly feminine spirit can be sensed by anyone in the atmosphere whether they are feminine or not. If it quacks like a duck, barks like a dog, meows like a cat, then...

This book was written with the desire that all women, including myself, become purely feminine, pure by femininity, and be the purest form of femininity.

One Last Note: I am not a licensed medical practitioner nor would I ever want to be. I, myself am not attempting to cure anything, but only in the Name of Jesus, do I share natural remedies that may alleviate anything you may be adversely experiencing. It is possible, with all the dynamics of the science and art of life, that you will feel better and great after doing the activities I suggest. Yet, please monitor your own thresholds of what you can and cannot physically, mentally, and spiritually do. Thank you for giving me and opportunity to assist you in your feminine journey!

Love ♥ ,

Olive Swan

August 7, 2019

Beach City in Southern California

POPULATION:

©thefeminineprincess™

There are many Girly Feminine Women. This

is because it is the entryway to true and full

femininity. Many women enter, but stay at the

11

entrance, not realizing there is so much more to femininity than girliness.

Then there are some Sensual Feminine Women. Several women have actually broken through the limitations of girliness and found their place in the world. They are extremely confident in their womanhood and many people admire their sexiness and still others are turned off by it due to envy. These have arrived at the highest point in the natural world that one can go.

Finally, there are even fewer Spiritual Feminine Women. These are able to operate in both the lower levels of Femininity at will, but remain constant and rooted at the highest level. They realize their femininity is a gift to bless others and to be an ambassador on earth for the heavenly Lord. They do not use it for self-gain, as the other two levels might do. They are called to a higher purpose and usually excel in it. This level flows in total trust in God, in His directions in her life, and in her God-given talents to permeate her assigned sphere. This is the highest level that reaches to, and extends, the spiritual realm of God.

CHARACTERISTICS

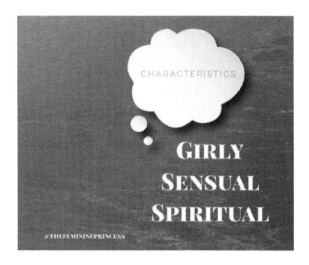

GIRLY GIRLS usually have pink and white theme-based decor. They are very youthful no matter what their actual age is. Even though they are very innocent, they can be very into themselves and their girly world. These girls dress in cute white and or pink colored dresses and smell very floral or fruity most of the time.

SENSUAL WOMEN pleasantly appeal to all of your senses at once. They smell like sultry, earthy, and musk-like scents. These women may or not wear a dress, but the way they move is very accentuating to their slightly sexual soul. They are very flirtatious and playful and may use a bit of girliness at will. They can also manipulate the energy and environment around them very well.

SPIRITUAL FEMMES are ethereal. Their divine nature causes many to question if they have just met and angel or not. These femmes are very mature and wise as they flow with the life they and God created together. She is able to use girliness or sensuality for an altruistic cause. Being ultra-confidence about her purpose in life, she is certain about her abilities and skill. Nothing shakes her healthy self-esteem. I did not mention what she wears because it doesn't matter; her nature, poise, disposition, and qualities clothe her, although she certainly doesn't look masculine.

TEMPERAMENT

A GIRLY GIRL WILL

a. Laugh a lot, for no obvious reason, at any moment

b. Dress and look adorably 'cute'

c. Squeal at exciting things

d. Have the diction of pop culture

e. Pick things that ooze 'girly'

f. Articulate in higher octaves

g. Has quick but gentle or dainty gestures

h. Eat sugar, candy, sweets, pies, cakes, cookies, etc.

A SENSUAL WOMAN WILL

a. Have a quiet seductive look in her eyes

b. Speak slowly at a lower pitched octave

c. Always stand, move, and walk in deliberate ways that accentuate her curves and body

d. Know herself well and is confident in every part of who she is

e. Draw people to her seductive energy

f. Wear her hair long and free

g. Promote love and sensuous living

h. Enjoy both savory and sweet foods but watches the gluten, flour, sugar ingredients

A SPIRITUAL FEMME WILL

a. Constantly observe people, awaiting to assist anyone who asks for, or appears to need help.

b. Look nice and neat but does not appear to be a glamour girl

c. Not need any outside validation as she is ultra-confident about her purpose in the earth and who she is in relation to it

d. Does not feel envy nor jealous but desires the best for everyone, including other attractive females

e. Has inner and outer beauty that everyone experiences that comes in contact with her

f. Can appear surreal-like, airy, and divine with her mannerisms, responses, and ideology

g. Celebrates, protects and endorses life at every level, for every living being

h. Understands the important of fresh, live foods for a healthy quality of life and attempts to stay away from harmful ingredients such as corn syrup, alcohol, sugar, white-flour based products, sodium, grease, etc.

GIRLY THEME: I'm so pretty: everyone please look at me! I'll use my femininity to attract many men. They'll desire me and I'll have my pick!

This is very immature because it neglects to take a myriad of factors into place and mostly centers on self.

SENSUAL THEME: I'm very attractive: men, let's connect and do something interesting! I'll use my femininity to attract the right man for me, the one I believe is for me.

This leans to human understanding, which is limited to experiences she's had up till now, her perception on life, past, and capacity to understand concepts and truths.

SPIRITUAL THEME: I've been given the gift of femininity and beauty: family, friends, even strangers, I will share it with you! I'll use my femininity to glorify God and trust that He will bring the one He has chosen from me in his timing.

This is the purest and highest form

of femininity, because of the focus is on the

Will and Way of the Creator. She is generous,

charitable, and considerate of all above

herself.

FEMININE LEVEL QUIZ:

Keep in mind this quiz is to give you some idea of where you may be positioned in femininity. You may already know and choose to skip the quiz. It is not necessary and the quiz is not absolute. This is to show you some idea which of the levels you vibe with the most. You may be more than one of these for different parts of your life, but you'll have one that dominates your persona. You may be in the middle of metamorphosing to another level. In truth you are! The proof is the very evidence of this book being in your hands. You are desiring to learn and grow and change. You will do so in every way, in appearance, in ego, in heart, in intelligence, in unconscious, and in spirit. Now take the test:

1. **What color(s) are you drawn to the most:** <u>a.</u> Pastels, especially pink <u>b.</u> Rich colors like purple, magentas, deep blues, rich greens, and black

c. Any color because you know how to wear them well

2. **What are some activities you enjoy doing:** a. Anything with a group of like-minded girls b. Something that appears to feeds your soul c. You select your events carefully based on its purpose, efficiency, and yield

3. **Your Best Gifts to receive:**

a. Anything pretty, especially teddy bears, stationary, candy b. Anything useful for women and has a touch a class or is of a classic style c. Anything pretty, useful, and classy that fits in your decor themes

4. **Your Dream Career is:** <u>a.</u> Working for any design, apparel, or accessories company that is cute / pretty <u>b.</u> Being a travel writer or blogger <u>c.</u> You have created your own enterprise

5. **Your Faith & Believe System includes:** <u>a.</u> New Age thinking <u>b.</u> Adopting ideologies here and there that fit with your personal philosophy <u>c.</u> Ancient, original, and tested in a monotheistic ruled world and universe

6. **Music and Movies that you prefer:** <u>a.</u> Chick flicks and pretty ballads by women <u>b.</u> Romance films and male group crooners <u>c.</u> Epic films / Period pieces about kingdoms

and positive music that nourishes your soul, intellect, and spirit

7. **Your friends:** a. Are just like you b. Are varied, but you share at least one to two things in common c. Are very few, but are cherished, devoted, and intimate confidants

8. **You like to receive new information:** a. With lots of pictures, graphics, and diagrams b. With a mixture of visuals and auditory channels and possibly another learning style or two c. With as many learning tools as possible (kinesthetic, naturalistic, spatial, audio, musical, logical, interpersonal, & interpersonal)

with no preference, as you can process

any information and interpret it when

and where needed

Tally up to your Score. Did you get:

Mostly As? Then you are GIRLY

Mostly Bs? Then you are SENSUAL

Mostly Cs? Then you are SPIRITUAL

Are you where you want to be? Use the rest

of this book to help get you there and keep

you there.

SENSORY ACTIVITIES

These activities were created to give you a taste of how artistic expression and sensory play can be therapeutic, while allowing room for growth and improvement. Take a tour of each level of femininity and explore each thoroughly that you may have them all in you, comprising and embodying femininity in its fullness. First let's begin with a prayer.

Prayer for the 3 Levels of Femininity™:

Father,

I desire to become a woman at the highest level

of femininity, which is really the best version of

myself as a woman, that you made and

planned since you created her at the beginning.

I chose your ideal strategy for my life. Walk

me through all the stages of femininity, if I

haven't gone through them already, and help

me excel in each one of them, remaining at the

top. I am willing to be an example, a symbol,

a paradigm for femininity in my immediate

community and for your greater purpose with

my life. I will sow good seeds of kindness,

thankfulness, and cheerfulness to You first

(not your creation, nor the universe) and those

You send to assist me on my journey.

In Jesus Name, Amen.

Key to the Following Activities:

❀ Girly

♡ Sensual

♔ Spiritual

Seeing (with the Art Modalities of

Collaging and Coloring):

❀ Take a girly image you admire or relish.

Collect five more images either from online,

magazine, or photos. Cut them out and

arrange them around the girly image on a

blank sheet of paper or a ledger in a journal.

Notice anything? Do the pictures you've

chosen speak to your past, your present or your future? This is where your mind is residing. Why is your mindset here? Next fill the background (or leave it blank) with color by marker, colored pens or pencils, watercolor or stamps. What color or colors, were you drawn to? Research the meaning of the colors you used and reflect on its relevance in your life. Once completed, place your collage on the wall, fridge or bulletin board where you can see it daily. What does it tell you each day? Something different or the same? Is its message applicable to your life now?

♡ Take a sensual image you admire or relish. Collect five more images either from online, magazine, or photos. Cut them out and arrange them around the sensual image on a blank sheet of paper or a ledger in a journal. Notice anything? Do the pictures you've chosen speak to your past, your present or your future? This is where your mind is residing. Why is your mindset here? Next fill the background (or leave it blank) with color by marker, colored pens or pencils, watercolor or stamps. What color or colors, were you drawn to? Research the meaning of the colors you used and reflect on its relevance in your life. Once completed, place your collage on the wall, fridge or bulletin board where you can see it daily. What does it tell you each day?

Something different or the same? Is its message applicable to your life now?

♔ Take a spiritual image you admire or relish. Collect five more images either from online, magazine, or photos. Cut them out and arrange them around the spiritual image on a blank sheet of paper or a ledger in a journal. Notice anything? ? Do the pictures you've chosen speak to your past, your present or your future? This is where your mind is residing. Why is your mindset here? Next fill the background (or leave it blank) with color by marker, colored pens or pencils, watercolor or stamps. What color or colors, were you drawn to? Research the meaning of the colors you used and reflect on its relevance in your

life. Once completed, place your collage on

the wall, fridge or bulletin board where you

can see it daily. What does it tell you each day?

Something different or the same? Is its

message applicable to your life now?

Hearing (with the Art Modalities of Music, Writing, & Journaling):

❀ Pick a slow tempo song by a female soloist. Listen to the whole track and then pick out a stanza that speaks to you. Write the verse or chorus down and meditate on it for a minute. Now add, alter, or omit it as much as you want to reflect more of your story, sentiment, and spirit. Reread your final version and write or type it out. Paste, post, or put it up where you can pay tribute to your personal stanza. Next record yourself voicing your special lines and listen to it once a day for the next seven days. Pay attention and record how it makes you feel. Does it change your mood at any given time and day? Does it still sound like your memoir or was it a passing fantasy?

♡ Pick a soft love song by an all-male band. Listen to the whole track and then pick out a stanza that speaks to you. Write the verse or chorus down and meditate on it for a minute. Now add, alter, or omit it as much as you want to reflect more of your story, sentiment, and spirit. Reread your final version and write or type it out. Paste, post, or put it up where you can pay tribute to your personal stanza. Next record yourself voicing your special lines and listen to it once a day for the next seven days. Pay attention and record how it makes you feel. Does it change your mood at any given time and day? Does it still sound like your memoir or was it a passing fantasy?

♕ Pick an upbeat positive song. Listen to the whole track and then pick out a stanza that speaks to you. Write the verse or chorus down and meditate on it for a minute. Now add, alter, or omit it as much as you want to reflect more of your story, sentiment, and spirit.

Reread your final version and write or type it out. Paste, post, or put it up where you can pay tribute to your personal stanza. Next record yourself voicing your special lines and listen to it once a day for the next seven days. Pay attention and record how it makes you feel. Does it change your mood at any given time and day? Does it still sound like your memoir or was it a passing fantasy?

Smelling (with the Art Modalities of

Aromatic, Naturopathy):

❀ Select your favorite girly perfume, essential oil, or scent (choose from possible fragrances of floral, fruity, citrus, sweet & warm, mints). If it is not already mixed with oil, use a carrier oil to mix the essence with the oil. After bathing for the next several days, use the blend to give yourself a self-massage, starting with the area of your body that needs it the most. Throughout the day inhale a whiff of your scented oil to bring you back to a place and dimension of girliness and relaxation.

♡ Select your favorite sensuous perfume, essential oil, or scent (choose from possible fragrances of spicy, woody, tobacco, musk, oriental, nutty). If it is not already mixed with oil, use a carrier oil to mix the essence with the oil. After bathing for the next several days, use the blend to give yourself a self-massage, starting with the area of your body that needs it the most. Throughout the day inhale a whiff of your scented oil to bring you back to a place and dimension of sensuality and relaxation.

♛ Select your favorite ethereal perfume, essential oil, or scent (choose from possible fragrances of oud, herbal, smoky, marine, earthy, airy, ancient). If it is not already mixed with oil, use a carrier oil to mix the essence with the oil. After bathing for the next several days, use the blend to give yourself a self-massage, starting with the area of your body that needs it the most. Throughout the day inhale a whiff of your scented oil to bring you back to a place and dimension of spirituality and relaxation.

Touching (with the Art Modalities of Play and Water):

❀ choose your favorite body of water and be creative! Think of a small sized body for girliness like a pond, puddle, or mist. If possible, go to the source of one – if not, find a video or a picture of one. Now list three ways it blesses us. Ponder how it produces something good for us. Now find a way to play with it – pulse a rhythm within, skip in or around it, splash it everywhere, really let yourself delve into girliness through the water.

♡ choose your favorite body of water and be creative! Think of a medium sized body for sensuality like a river, stream, or fountain. If possible, go to the source of one – if not, find a video or a picture of one. Now list three ways it blesses us. Ponder how it produces something good for us. Now find a way to play with it – pour it on yourself, dance in or around it, wet nearby rocks, really let yourself delve into your sensuality through the water.

♛ choose your favorite body of water and be creative! <u>Think of a vast sized body for sensuality like a waterfall, sea, or rainstorm.</u> If possible, go to the source of one – if not, find a video or a picture of one. Now list three ways it blesses us. Ponder how it produces something good for us. Now find a way to play with it – make waves with it a rhythm within, twirl in or around it, get a veil or scarf to dance with it, really let yourself delve into spirituality through water.

Tasting (with the Art Modalities of

Herbalism, Aroma, & Horticulture):

❀ Name one area in girliness you may need

healing in. Find an herb, a spice, and a flower

that would relieve your aliment. You may

need to do on online search for this if you do

not own any books on the subject. Decide on

a dish or meal that would incorporate these

components. Cook the recipe. Don't forgot to smell your dish as it's cooking and when eating it. As you nibble on each bite, consider the healing properties your meal is bringing to that area in your life. Over the next week, observe any changes in that area as well as the speed, intensity, and range the healing takes place. You may need to repeat this process a quite a few times to see lasting results.

♡ Name one area in sensuality you may need healing in. Find an herb, a spice, and a flower that would relieve your aliment. You may need to do on online search for this if you do not own any books on the subject. Decide on a dish or meal that would incorporate these components. Prepare the recipe. Don't forgot to smell your dish as it's cooking and when eating it. As you dine on each morsel, meditate the healing properties your meal is bringing to that plane in your life. Over the next week, observe any changes in that plane as well as the speed, intensity, and range the healing takes place. You may need to repeat this process a quite a few times to see lasting results.

♔ Name one area in spirituality you may need healing in. Find an herb, a spice, and a flower that would relieve your aliment. You may need to do on online search for this if you do not own any books on the subject. Decide on a dish or meal that would incorporate these components. Arrange the recipe. Don't forgot to smell your dish as it's cooking and when eating it. As you banquet on each portion, celebrate the healing properties your meal is bringing to that realm in your life. Over the next week, observe any changes in that realm as well as the speed, intensity, and range the healing takes place. You may need to repeat this process a quite a few times to see lasting results.

Feeling (with the Art Modalities of Movement, Dance, & Drama):

❀ Focus on feeling girly – youthful, sweet, and innocent. Envision how a girly girl would act, behave and move. For one day, if you aren't already her, pretend to be her all day.

Do everything and converse with everyone in the manner she would. Be playful, young and silly, but sweet. Stay in character no matter what happens or who questions you. When you are alone, start dancing, with or without music, how you believe a girly girl would dance. If you are clueless, get some ideas on YouTube!

♡ Focus on feeling sensual – sexual, seductive, and subtle. Envision how a sensual woman would act, behave and move. For one day, if you aren't already her, pretend to be her all day. Do everything and converse with everyone in the manner she would. Be confident, alluring, classy, and flirty, but subtle and respectable. Stay in character no matter what happens or who questions you. When you are alone, start dancing, with or without music, how you believe a sensual woman would dance. If you are clueless, get some ideas on YouTube!

♛ Focus on feeling spiritual – angelic, holy, and pure. Envision how a spiritual angel would act, behave and move. For one day, if you aren't already her, pretend to be her all day. Do everything and converse with everyone in the manner she would. Be natural, authentic and perfect, but godly. Stay in character no matter what happens or who questions you. When you are alone, start dancing, with or without music, how you believe a spiritual angel would dance. If you are clueless, get some ideas on YouTube!

Thinking (with the Art Modalities of Mindfulness, Nature-immersion, & Bibliography):

❀ Pack a beauty or home decor book or magazine to view and go to a park. Concentrate on the present, name everything that is happening to all your senses at that moment. What do you see? What do you hear? What do you smell? What do you taste? What can you feel? Next think about a good friend joining you and how she might interact with your current scene. She is offering you pink cotton candy, sheer lip-gloss, and a pretty pink and white polka dotted dress. How do you respond? Do all of your senses change perception?

♡ Pack a book or magazine about the human body or forms of entertainment to read and go to a beach. Concentrate on the present, name everything that is happening to all your senses at that moment. What do you see? What do you hear? What do you smell? What do you taste? What can you feel? Next think about a handsome man approaching you and how that might interact with your current location. He desires to buy you a Lebanese dinner, take you to a live jazz band, and purchase you an outfit for the occasion. How do you respond? Do all of your senses change perception?

♔ Pack a book or magazine about wisdom, proverbs, or famous quotes to study and go to a forest or the mountains. Concentrate on the present, name everything that is happening to all your senses at that moment. What do you see? What do you hear? What do you smell? What do you taste? What can you feel? Next think about being surrounded with beautiful celestial heavenly bodies and how that might interact with your current landscape. They are beckoning you to take a supernatural trip to space with your memory, appearance, and insides intact the whole way. How do you respond? Do all of your senses change perception?

Dreaming (with the Art Modalities of Guided Imagery, Spirituality & Symbolism):

❀ Picture yourself in an ideal girly atmosphere. Where are you? What are you doing? Is there anyone with you? What are you wearing? How do you feel? Can you share as many details about your vision as possible?

Now picture someone you greatly respect, admire, have obeisance to, and or seek counsel from, next to you. You have one minute to do or discuss anything with this person. What do you choose and why? Keenly see any objects, things, or goods in that environment. What do they mean to you?

♡ Picture yourself in an ideal sensual atmosphere. Where are you? What are you doing? Is there anyone with you? What are you wearing? How do you feel? Can you share as many details about your vision as possible? Now picture someone you greatly respect, admire, have obeisance to, and or seek counsel from next to you. You have one minute to do or discuss anything with this person. What do you choose and why? Keenly see any objects, things, or goods in that environment. What do they mean to you?

♔ Picture yourself in an ideal spiritual atmosphere. Where are you? What are you doing? Is there anyone with you? What are you wearing? How do you feel? Can you share as many details about your vision as possible? Now picture someone you greatly respect, admire, have obeisance to, and or seek counsel from next to you. You have one minute to discuss or do anything with this person. What do you choose and why? Keenly see any objects, things, or goods in that

environment. What do they mean to you?

Saying (with the Art Modalities of

Instrumentation):

❀ Get a wind or stringed instrument, a flute,

small guitar, sitar, or shamisen. If you don't

know how to play it, find some basic rhythm

patterns online and learn them as quickly as

you can. Afterward, speak or sing some lyrics

from your heart that coincide with the

instrument, melody, and girliness. Regard the words that flow from your lips. Do they flow easily or are they challenging form? Why do you think that is so? What topics are you centering on? What emotion is at your core? Are you enjoying yourself? How do you feel today? Did anything happen to influence you and your words today? If they are not already so, can you transform them to something powerful, meaningful, positive, and optimistic?

♡ Get a percussion instrument, like the triangle, tambourine, or drums. If you don't know how to play it, find some basic rhythm patterns online and learn them as quickly as you can. Afterward, speak or sing some lyrics from your heart that coincide with the instrument, melody, and sensuality. Regard the words that flow from your lips. Do they flow easily or are they challenging form? Why do you think that is so? What topics are you centering on? What emotion is at your core? Are you enjoying yourself? How do you feel today? Did anything happen to influence you and your words today? If they are not already so, can you transform them to something powerful, meaningful, positive, and optimistic?

♟ Get a stringed or percussion instrument, like finger cymbals, a harp, or violin. If you don't know how to play it, find some basic rhythm patterns online and learn them as quickly as you can. Afterward, speak or sing some lyrics from your heart that coincide with the instrument, melody, and spirituality. Regard the words that flow from your lips. Do they flow easily or are they challenging form? Why do you think that is so? What topics are you centering on? What emotion is at your core? Are you enjoying yourself? How do you feel today? Did anything happen to influence you and your words today? If they are not already so, can you transform them to something powerful, meaningful, positive, and optimistic?

TRIPLE DECLARATIONS

I have declarations I've written to speak over your life that the Lord gave me for you, to bless you. They can easily be turned into affirmations, once you've declared them, by substituting 'You' for 'I' with the corresponding verb form. If you are not yet ready to recite them aloud, that's ok too. Only proceed when you feel ready. You may elect to focus on one level at a time for a week and allow the statements to penetrate your soul. Each level has its distinct advantages, so you don't want to skip the lower ones. Remember, the spiritual feminine woman, has them all.

GIRLY:

I anoint you (by the authority I was given, I share the gift that was given to me), with the spirit of girly femininity. I declare You are becoming more and more girly by the second of each day. You will walk, talk, think, and move in girliness all the time. You are a girly girl from your DNA to your personal energetic magnetic field. Your emotions, heart, and mind, are sound and strengthened in being a girl. Both men and women are greatly and positively affected by your girliness and are indirectly influenced by you. Your body is shaped, formed and created in girliness. You are smart, cute, and lovely. All your movements and gestures are extremely femininely girly and are soft and smooth. You laugh, speak, utter in a sweet girly manner. Your attitude is youthful, expressive, and positive. When you walk into a room, your aura proclaims: Girly! These declarations are having good and positive changes and transitions in your life and are permanently effective. You will have no adverse effect, evil repercussion, nor bad incident because of these statements. You are receiving everything out of the universe a girl could want, sent to you by God. You are thankful for all the wonderful transformations that are taking place by Christ Jesus. You bless the Lord with your response to these alterations of good in your life. You are getting revelation and illumination on how God will purpose you in girliness. The Holy Spirit is rapidly and safely doing these beneficial changes of girly feminine loveliness.

SENSUAL:

I anoint you (by the authority I was given, I share the gift that was given to me) with the spirit of sensual femininity. I declare You are becoming more and more sensual by the second of each day. You will walk, talk, think, and move in sensuousness all the time. You are a sensual woman from your DNA to your personal energetic magnetic field. Your emotions, heart, and mind, are sound and strengthened in being a woman. Both men and women are greatly and positively affected by your sensual-ness and are directly impacted by you. You love yourself completely and wholly. You are perfectly designed by the Creator with a unique personality, rare traits, gorgeous physique, and impressive intellect. You can easily accept others and their uniqueness because you love yourself. Your body is shaped, formed, and created in sensuality. Your appearance is radiating health and brightness. You are attractive, compelling, and appealing. All your movements and gestures are extremely and femininely sensuous as well as slow and sensual. Your posture and body language ooze femininity. You laugh, speak, utter in a seductive manner. You stay in perfect ideal shape for life. When you walk into a room, your aura proclaims: Sensual! You are open at all times, to connect with the right people destined to be in your life. These declarations are having good and positive changes and transitions in your life and are permanently effective. You will have no adverse effect, evil repercussion, nor bad incident because of these statements. You are receiving everything out of the universe a woman could want, sent to you by God. You are thankful for all the wonderful

transformations that are taking place by Christ

Jesus. You bless the Lord with your response

to these alterations of good in your life. You

are getting revelation and illumination on how

God will purpose you in sensuality. The Holy

Spirit is rapidly and safely doing these

beneficial changes of sensual feminine

prettiness.

SPIRITUAL:

I anoint you (by the authority I was given, I

share the gift that was given to me) with the

spirit of spiritual femininity. I declare You are

becoming more and more divinely spiritual by

the second of each day. You will walk, talk,

think, and move in divine spirituality all the

time. You are a divine woman from your

DNA to your personal energetic magnetic

field. Your emotions, heart, and mind, are

sound and strengthened in being a godly

woman. Both men and women are greatly and

positively affected by your spirit and are

moved to change by you. Your spirit is

shaped, formed and created in divine

goodness. Your appearance is radiating the

face and goodness of God. You are angelic,

generous, and loving. All your movements

and gestures are extremely femininely divine

as well as deliberate and altruistic. Your

posture and body language ooze femininity.

Your face and body are ultra-feminine

looking. You laugh, speak, utter in a full, free,

and expressive manner. You love yourself completely and wholly and are able capable of loving others equally. You are perfectly designed, inside and out, by the Creator with a pleasing personality, rare traits, stunning physique, and extraordinary intellect. You can easily perceive other's uniqueness and accept their limitations. You stay in perfect ideal shape for life while your mind is consistently exercised and stimulated to create new neurons to stay mentally agile. When you walk into a room, your aura proclaims: Spiritual! Your steps are ordered of God and you are always at the right place and at the right time, and with the right people that is part of your destiny. You are constantly improving and preparing yourself for any opportunity the Lord brings you and for the ones you've been asking for and or secretly desiring. These declarations are having good and positive changes and transitions in your life and are permanently effective. You will have no adverse effect, evil repercussion, nor bad incident because of these statements. You are receiving everything out of the universe a celestial being could want, sent to you by God, in order that you may give much to others. For the glory and works of God, you are magnetic and admired, that His divine assignments may be completed in, by, and through you. The environment, events, and actions surrounding you are working for His purpose and your greater good. You are filled with great peace and bring peace with you wherever you go, knowing that He is your peace and you can trust Him at all times, through every circumstance, and with each progression in your life. You stay humble and consider others as you do for yourself. Your life is valuable and has meaning as it is shared for a sacred consecration by the Lord. He fills you with joy as you think of and celebrate others. You too shall be filled as you fill others, providing what you can and what is needed. All your relationships are a gift from God and are mutually beneficial. You receive everything you need to fulfill your assignment on this earth. You excel in social and communication skills and are sharpened in your craft. You are thankful for all the wonderful transformations that are taking place by Christ Jesus. You bless the Lord with your response to these alterations of good in your life and those you touch. You are getting revelation and illumination on how God will purpose you in spirituality. Your instincts are acutely sensitive to the Holy Spirit and your heart is under and obedience and guidance of Him. The Holy Spirit is rapidly and safely doing these beneficial changes of spiritual feminine beautifulness.

SPIRITUAL INSURANCE & COVENANT

If you've been reading this material and
currently are not connected to God, whose
Name is the Lord, Almighty, "I Am that I
Am", let's take this opportunity to rejoin
ourselves with Him. He desires to
communicate with you just like it was in the
beginning of time. There may be many paths
in life, but only one way to God, and that is
through His Son, Jesus Christ, (Yashua ben
Adonai, bey Ivrit) the Messiah of all nations.

To reconnect with Him is easy, yet powerful.
The Bible says in Romans Chapter 10, verses
9 & 10, that if you confess with your mouth

and believe in your Heart that God raised [Jesus] from the dead, you will be saved. Your heart's belief brings you to righteousness and your confession brings you salvation. Many have made Jesus their Savior, but not their Lord nor King. They believe in Him, but don't allow Him to be Lord and King over their lives by letting Him guide, teach, and direct them. To be Saved and dwell with Him for all eternity in Heaven, you must allow Him to be all three to you, according to Matthew 7:21-23.

If you declare this prayer out loud & sincerely believe it, you will truly come into His Kingdom and not a religion:

Oh Father,

Forgive my sin, for I was born into it. But I know you sent your only firstborn Son to come and die for me, in my place. He destroyed all the works of the enemy and gave me power to do so too. You raised Him from the dead, that I might have eternal life with You. I receive Him as my Savior, my Lord, and my King. Fill me with your Spirit and guide me in life to my purpose and destiny. Teach me to live for You and carry your nature. I love You and thank You for this opportunity to become one with you again.

In Jesus Name,

Amen

If you have prayed that in genuineness and out loud (both the natural and spiritual realms need to hear your decree, that's why when you are asked to make a vow or renounce something you must speak it audibly), then welcome to a Kingdom of righteousness, peace, and joy!! A Kingdom without end and with true abundance of love, pleasure, and life!

Write me at thefeminineprincess@gmail.com, if you prayed this, so I can send you a welcome gift for entering the family of Christ! Make sure you write in the subject field "Accepted Christ via your book (fill in the title)". Also, please notate if you are a Woman pursing femininity!

Start reading the Bible to learn His ways, surround yourself with similar minds, study related materials or media, and listen to praise / worship songs. Be cautious and ask the Spirit for discernment on what you watch, what you listen to, and who you hang around. The Lord will reveal truth, motives, and secrets to help your spiritual growth and the Holy Spirit will guide you away from any false way, if you are willing to follow Him.

ABOUT THE AUTHOR

Olive Swan is a Feminine Expressive Arts Consultant and a Professional member of the International Expressive Arts Therapy Association. She shares the depth of femininity through various art modalities. Olive takes pleasure in all things girly, sensual, and spiritual, most things pastel, and some things Mediterranean. She *wrote 33 Day*

Devotional for Feminine Women, _39 Elements of Femininity_, _How to Get & Keep a King_, _Olive or Olivia?_, _50 Best Dance Quotes_ to help others blossom in the spirit and energy of a feminine woman. She also held conference calls on various feminine topics that are now recorded for the general public.

She also wrote _7 Wealth Laws every believer should live by_ and _8 Timeless Lessons on Wealth_. Her artwork also reflects her spiritual interpretations and can be viewed and/or purchased at https://www.saatchiart.com/oliveswan.

Her quest to become ultra-feminine blossomed in 5775 (2014). Since then, she has studied feminine nature, women, girls, objects, books, colors, textiles, art, etc. Being more feminine has changed her approach to life, other people, as well as her decor. She believes being feminine is a high-class art that is available to all who wish it upon themselves.

Want to keep up to date with upcoming seminars, class, & workshops? Request to be added to our email list at connect@oliveswan.pink.

Want to work with a feminine consultant to explore more artistic ways to deepen and broaden your femininity? Request a session with me, a Feminine Expressive Art Consultant trained in the arts of femininity and the process of using the arts to grow at www.oliveswan.pink

Want a free e-book? Join our new 'Femininity Princess Community' and become a part of something great. We are a group of feminine women that believe in femininity and work to perfect it in our lives. When you sign up, you receive, my e-book "18 Ways to Become Feminine, Fast". Join at:

https://theffeminineprincess.com/free-e-book/.

Learn more about femininity, order our feminine goods, participate in our services, or send a request, suggestion, or comment by:

*main site:

www.oliveswan.pink

*blog site:

https://thefeminineprincess.com

*YouTube:

https://www.youtube.com/thefeminineprincess

*our store

https://oliveswan.pink/pink-peach-cream

*classes on CD:

https://oliveswan.pink/pink-peach-cream

*instagram:

http://instagram.com/thefeminineprincess

*pinterest:

https://www.pinterest.com/thefeminineprincess

*twitter:

https://twitter.com/feminineolive

*email:

thefeminineprincess@gmail.com

God Bless You and Your Feminine Journey! :-)

NOTES

DATE:

THEME:

NARRATIVE:

LEARNED:

GRATEFUL:

TASKS:

NOTES

DATE:

THEME:

NARRATIVE:

LEARNED:

GRATEFUL:

TASKS:

NOTES

DATE:

THEME:

NARRATIVE:

LEARNED:

GRATEFUL:

TASKS:

NOTES

DATE:

THEME:

NARRATIVE:

LEARNED:

GRATEFUL:

TASKS:

NOTES

DATE:

THEME:

NARRATIVE:

LEARNED:

GRATEFUL:

TASKS:

NOTES

DATE:

THEME:

NARRATIVE:

LEARNED:

GRATEFUL:

TASKS:

Printed in Great Britain
by Amazon